MW00885995

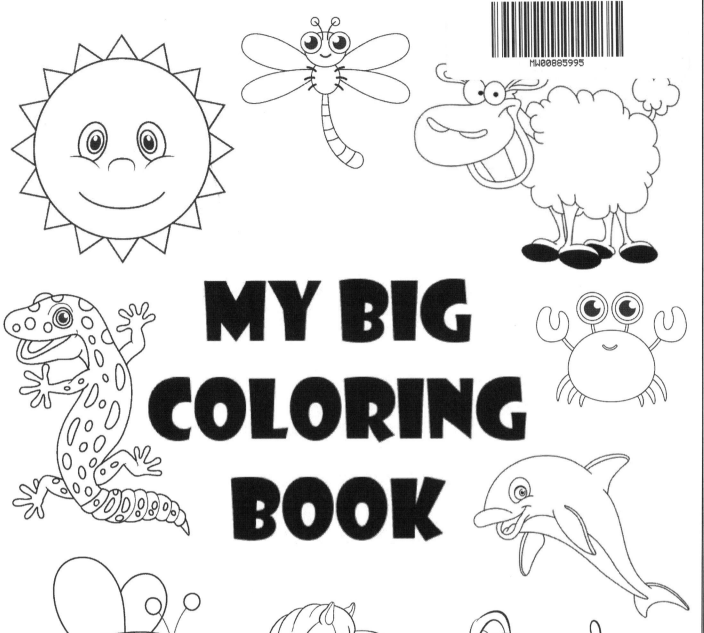

MY BIG COLORING BOOK

Copyright © 2023 by Happy Lion

ISBN: 9798371707529

All rights reserved. No part of this book may be reproduced or used in any manner without written permission of the copyright owner except for the use of quotations in a book review.

Lion

Cat

Tiger

Fox

Donkey

Camel

Sheep

Elephant

Kangaroo

Giraffe

Beaver

Squirrel

Crocodile

Panda

Leopard

Owl

Seal

Whale

Duck

Monkey

Turtle

Horse

Hippopotamus

Cow

Penguin

Gorilla

Shark

Starfish

Octopus

Frog

Crab

Dolphin

Flamingo

Eagle

Cricket

Swan

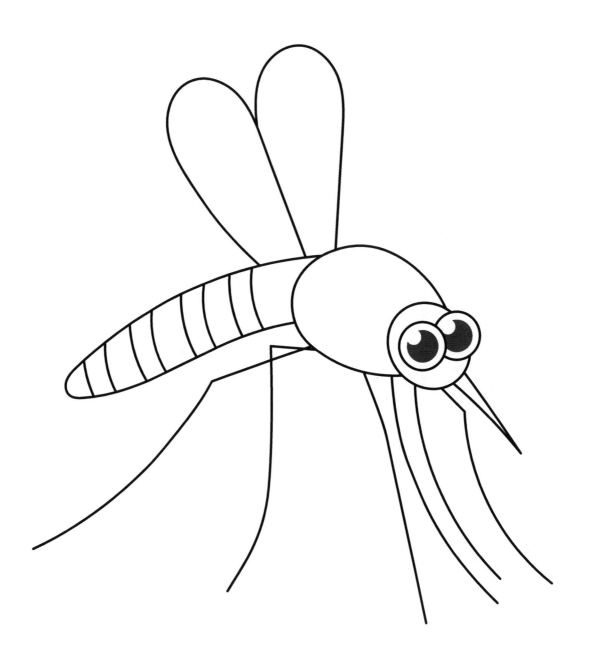

Mosquito

Caterpillar

Ant

Lizard

Snail

Dragonfly

Butterfly

Parrot

Hedgehog

Chick

Bat

Rooster

Mouse

Medusa

Hen

Snake

Sun

Rose

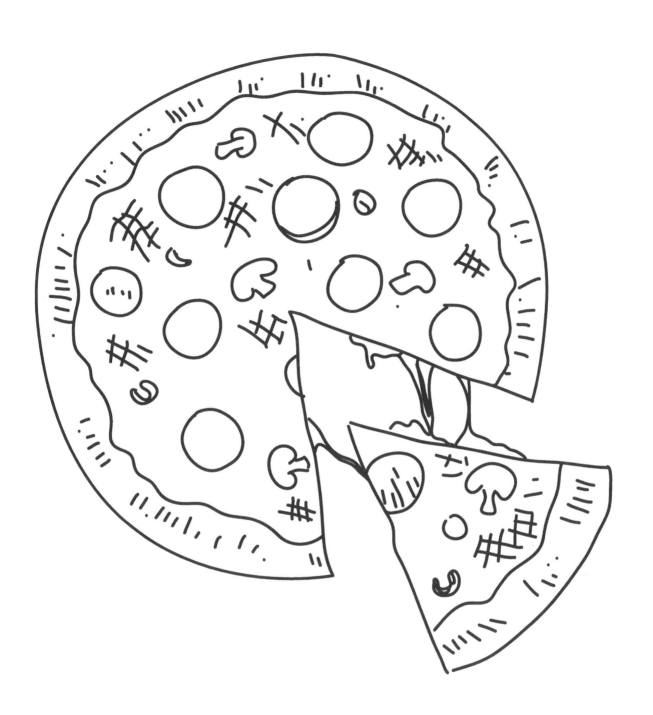

Pizza

Candy

Beehive

Balloons

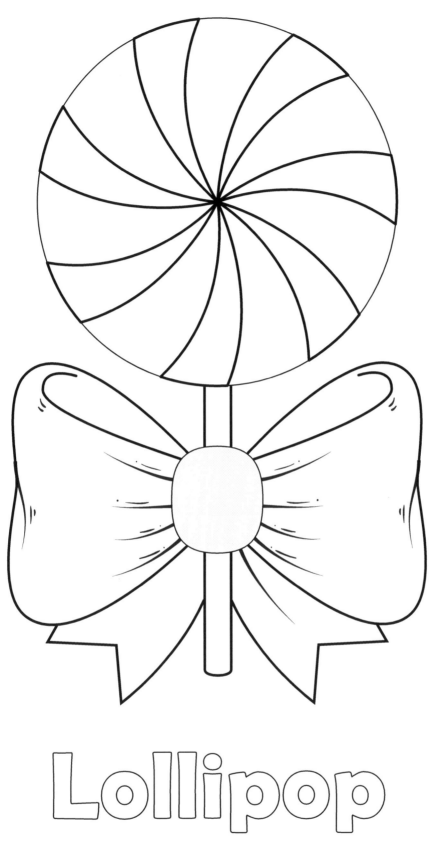

Lollipop

Ice cream

Cake

Doll

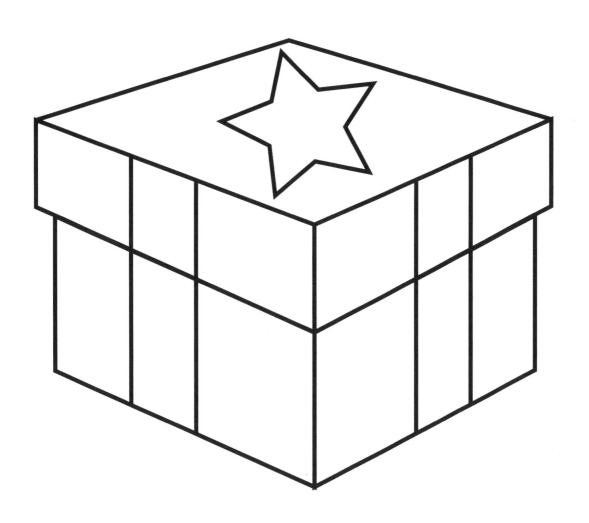

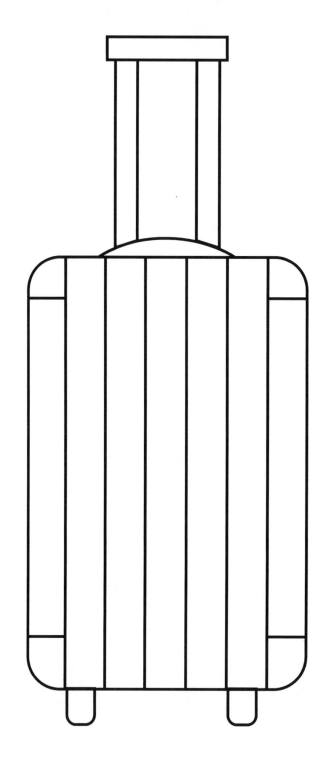

Suitcase

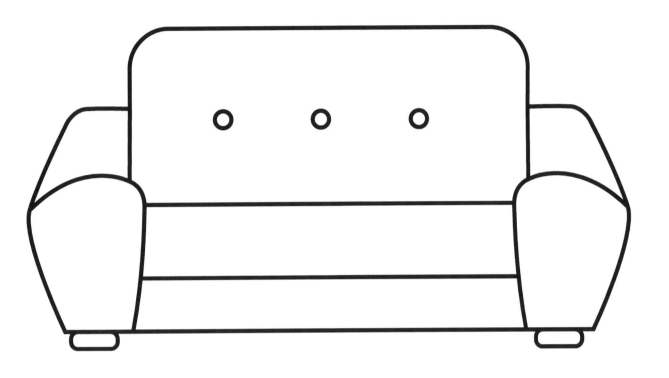

Sofa

Key

Cup

Carousel

Cloud

Glasses

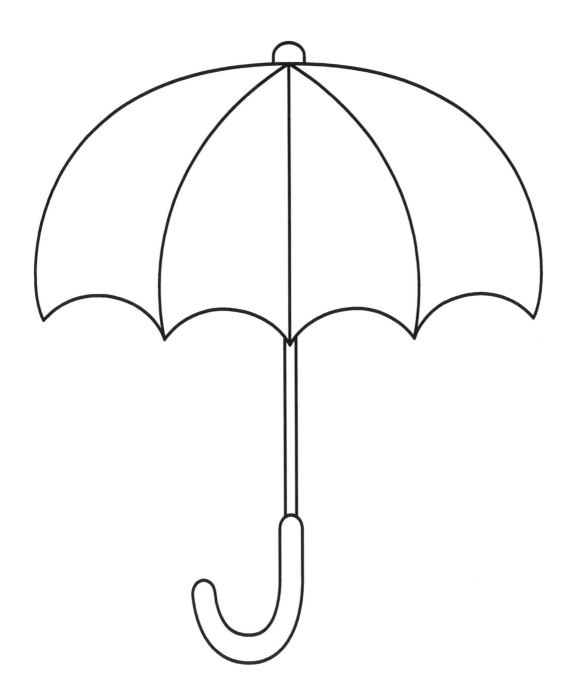

Umbrella

Bicycle

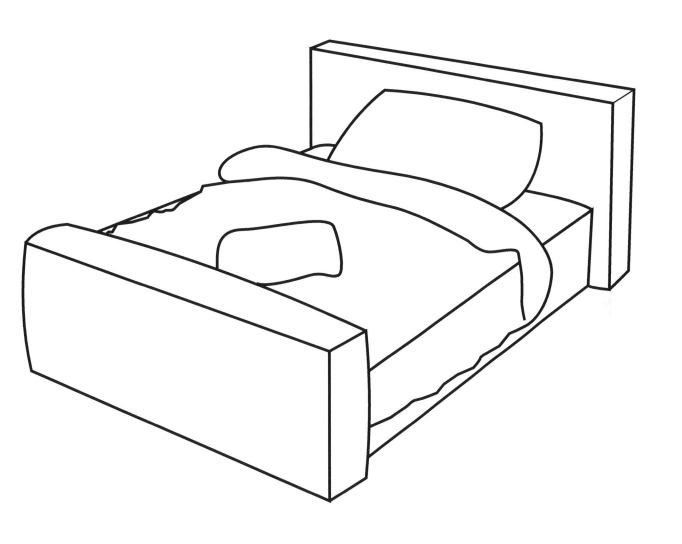

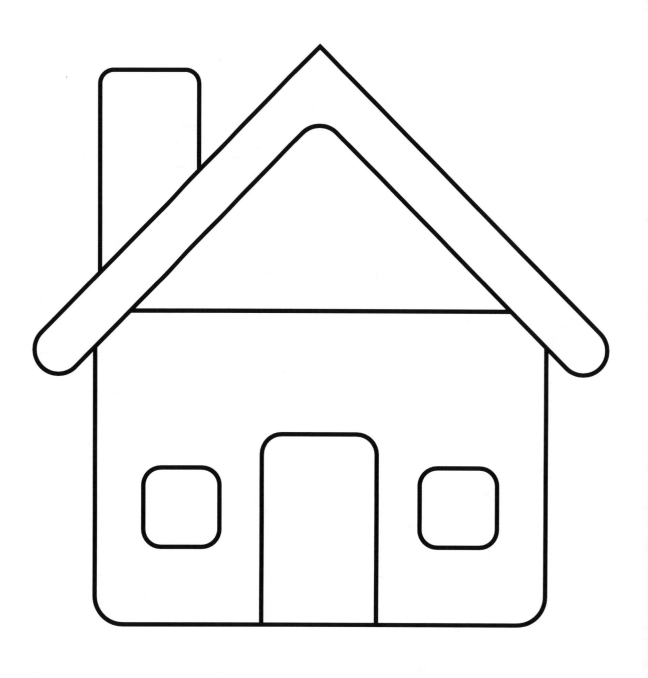

House

Boat

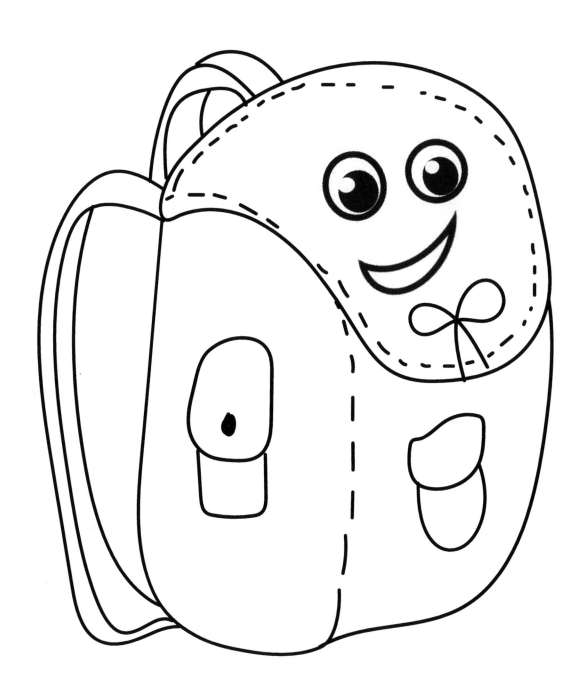

Bag

Blackboard

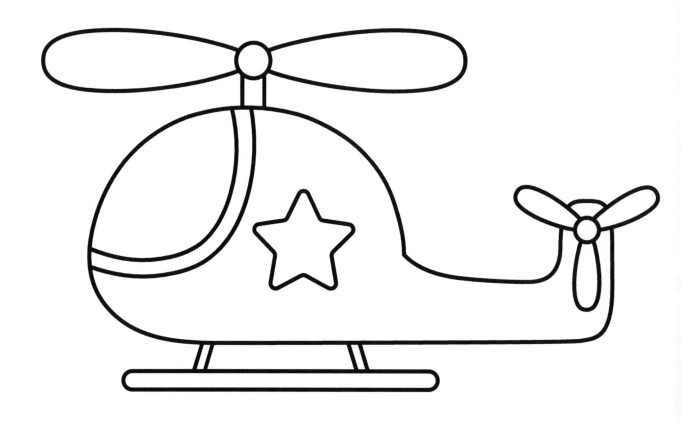

Helicopter

Hammer

Washing machine

Car

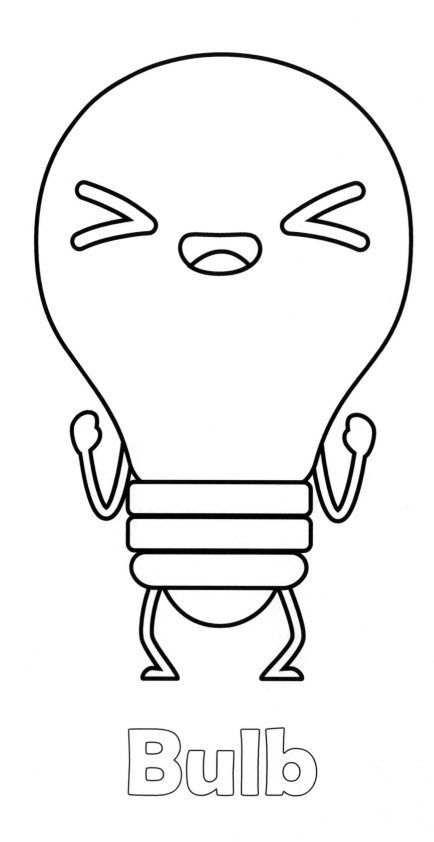

Bulb

Book

Shoes

Chair

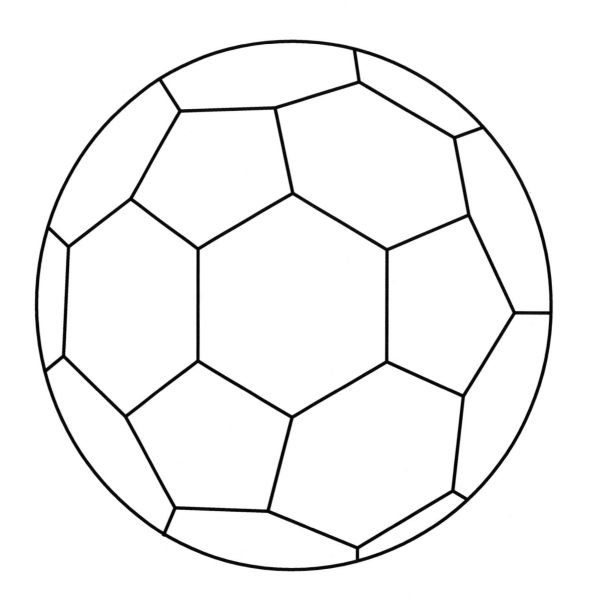

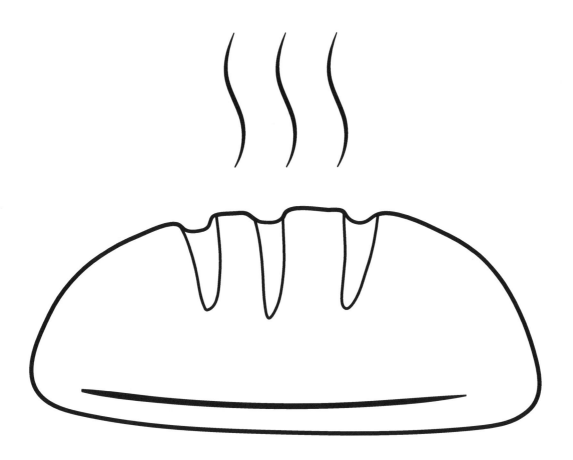

Bread

Clock

Plane

Guitar

Tractor

Pear

Apple

Pineapple

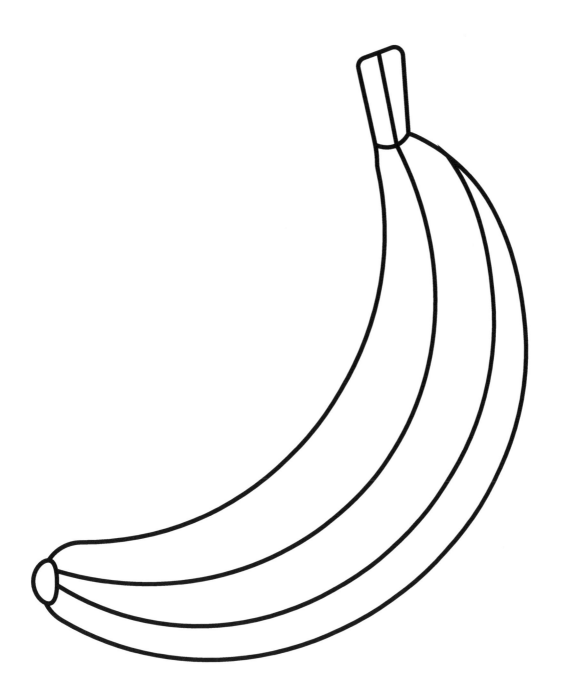

Banana

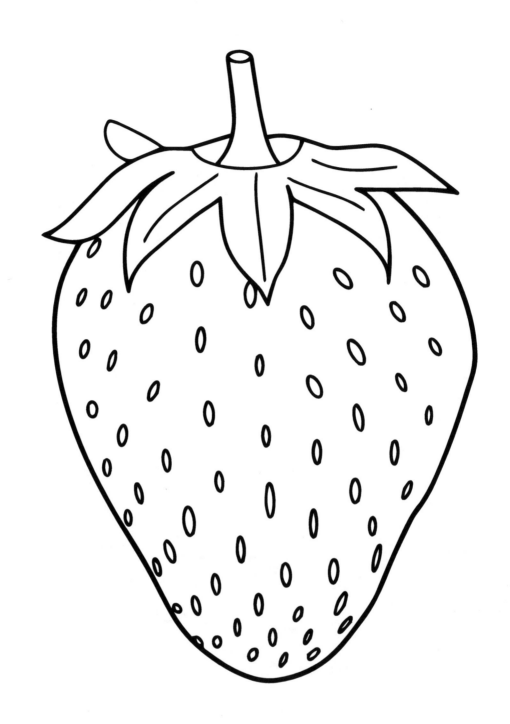

Strawberrie

Orange

Grapes

Cherries

Castle

Would you like to receive periodically educational books and free teaching material to entertain your child?

Then sign up for the FB group of Happy Lion children's books!

Scan the QR code you see on this page or type the following address:

https://www.facebook.com/groups/2882387582048536/

Scan this QR code.

Thanks from

Happy Lion

Made in the USA
Monee, IL
21 May 2024

58767263R00059